The Dyk
Branch Line

Peter A. Harding

D1 class 0-4-2T No.214, (formerly No.13 *Pimlico*) at the Dyke Station with the branch train in 1926.
The late J.E.Kite. Courtesy of B.R.Hart

Published by Peter A. Harding,
"Mossgiel", Bagshot Road, Knaphill,
Woking, Surrey GU21 2SG.

ISBN 0 9523458 5 4

Printed by Binfield Printers Ltd.,
Binfield Road, Byfleet, Surrey KT14 7PN.

Contents

Introduction	3	Timetables and Tickets	28
History of the Line	4	Closure	29
Description of the Route	17	The Present Scene	31
Motive Power and Rolling Stock	24	Conclusion	32
Operation	27	Acknowledgements/Bibliography	32

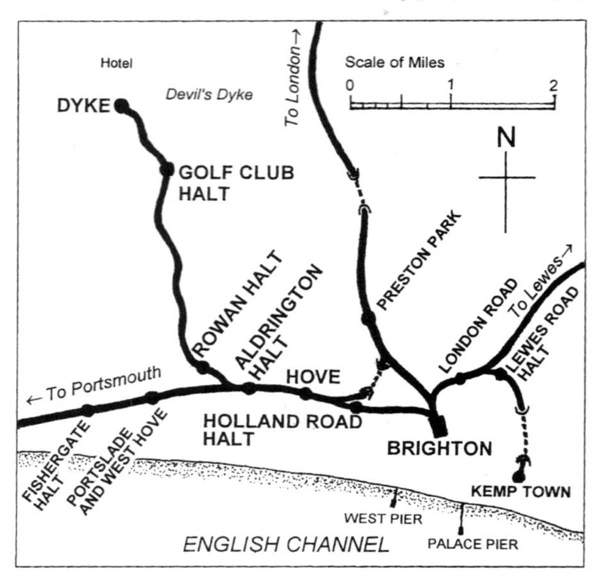

The Sentinel steam railbus at the Dyke Station. This vehicle worked the branch from May 1st 1933 until May 1st 1935. Lens of Sutton

Introduction

The Dyke branch line was opened by a private company known as the Brighton and Dyke Railway on September 1st 1887 to provide a ready means of access to the Devil's Dyke, a popular beauty spot situated on the South Downs to the north west of Brighton. The branch left the main Brighton - Portsmouth line at a junction to the west of Hove Station. It turned northwards climbing mainly up a 1 in 40 gradient before reaching the terminus which was just over $3\frac{1}{2}$ miles from the junction.

Although the London, Brighton & South Coast Railway never owned the line, they worked and maintained it from the opening, as well as providing all the rolling stock, for 55 per cent of the gross receipts. After the 1923 grouping, both the Brighton and Dyke Railway and the London, Brighton & South Coast Railway became part of the newly formed Southern Railway, who owned and worked the branch until it closed.

The traffic was mainly seasonal and depended very much on the weather, although in earlier years it was the only means of reaching the Devil's Dyke other than walking, or riding in a very bumpy horse drawn carriage or cart.

As the roads were improved and cars and buses became more popular, the little branch line lost it's main sauce of income and was closed completely on December 31st 1938.

I hope this booklet will give readers a chance to capture some of the irresistible charm of a railway from a bygone age when locomotives puffed and blew their way up the South Downs.

This booklet is dedicated to the late John L. Smith of "Lens of Sutton", who over the years has not only provided many of the photographs used in my booklets but also for many hundreds of other publications. *Peter A. Harding*

E4 class 0-6-2T No.2505 starts the journey back to Brighton with a single carriage train having just left the Dyke Station in 1938. The late O.J.Morris / Lens of Sutton

History of the Line

The legend of the Devil's Dyke, which is a deep ravine situated on the South Downs some five and a half miles to the north west of Brighton, and adjoining Dyke Hill which rises to 700 ft above sea level, has always fascinated local people and tourists alike, and added to the splendid views of the surrounding countryside, it is not so surprising that it became such a major attraction.

There are several versions from ancient folklore of how the area received its name but the most popular seems to be that the Devil was envious of the Wealden villages and churches which lay inland of the South Downs and he wanted to let in the sea and flood them by completing the ravine. Saint Cuthman of Steyning was the person who stopped him with the aid of an old lady who lit a taper while the Devil was preparing to do the evil deed before dawn. Seeing the light of the taper and mistaking it for the start of daylight, he quickly fled leaving his pick-axe and footprints as evidence.

To help the steady flow of visitors, a wooden hut was erected on Dyke Hill in 1818 to serve as an inn. This was replaced in 1831 by a small inn which was built on the site. As the years moved on this small inn was taken over by William Thacker who developed it into a proper hotel known appropriately as the Dyke Hotel and it was soon regarded as 'the place' to visit and attracted many famous people ranging from Queen Victoria to Rudyard Kipling. As the Dyke Hotel became more popular, the method of horse drawn transport or just plain walking was becoming a real problem.

In 1872 plans were drawn up by the proposed Brighton and Devil's Dyke Railway Company for a standard gauge railway line to run from the parish of Preston on the north side of what is now the Old Shoreham Road, to terminate 130 yards north west of the hotel in the parish of Poynings, after climbing gradients of as much as 1 in 44. The engineers for this proposed line were W.H.Le Feuvre and W.T.Carrington. Surprisingly, there were no plans to connect to the London Brighton & South Coast Railway (LBSCR), and it was probably this reason that the line was doomed from the start.

Although the Bill survived a first reading in the House of Commons on February 11th 1873 and was ordered to be committed after its second reading six days later, it was withdrawn due to a lack of support.

Later in the same year, the Brighton and Devil's Dyke Railway proposed two new lines, to try and decide which would be best. The engineers were now J.H.Tolmé and Charles O. Blaber. The first plan was similar to the previous one, but this time would connect with the LBSCR and start from the main Brighton - London line just south of Patcham Tunnel. The second plan would also connect with the LBSCR by commencing from a junction on the main Brighton - Portsmouth line in the parish of Hove, approximately 1 mile 69 chains from Brighton Station, and terminate south west of the Dyke Hotel. After some discussion, the promoters decided to proceed with the second plan which was to run from the junction on the main Brighton - Portsmouth line.

The Bill received its second reading on March 30th 1874, but like the first Bill in February 1873 it was also withdrawn, this time due to problems between the railway company and two landowners, Lord Leconfield and the Earl of Abergavenny.

In 1877 the same Bill was again promoted and this time the Brighton and Dyke Railway Act (note the word Devil's was removed from the title), dated August 2nd 1877 was successful in getting through Parliament. The newly formed Brighton and Dyke Railway Company (B&DR) was headed by William Hall, a Lancing gentleman, William John Smith, a Brighton wine merchant and William Hudson, a contractor from Brighton. Surprisingly, this new Act gave the B&DR powers to construct the line in two sections, the first from a junction with the LBSCR in the parish of Hove, at

1 mile 69 chains from Brighton Station and terminate in the parish of Hangleton after 3 miles 16 chains. This would be known as Railway No.1. The second line which would be known as Railway No.2, would connect with Railway No.1 by a junction in the parish of Hangleton and would continue 1 mile 50 chains to a terminus south of the Dyke Hotel. Eventually, the idea of a junction in the parish of Hangleton was dropped and the railway to the Dyke was constructed as one line.

The capital of the new B&DR was £72,000 with powers to issue debenture stock to the value of £24,000. The LBSCR were to decide exactly where the junction on their Brighton - Portsmouth line should be, and Lord Leconfield, who was one of the landowners who had proved to be a stumbling block over earlier plans was to be compensated. If required, the B&DR undertook to build three bridges and a 60 yard siding where the line was to pass through Lord Leconfield's estate. The period given for completion was to be five years and it was also stated that powers for compulsory purchase were not to be used after three years. Some of the land near the Dyke was the property of the Crown and was sold to the B&DR for £100 per acre, subject to an existing lease.

In 1882 the B&DR reached an agreement with the LBSCR to work and maintain the line and provide all the rolling stock for 55 per cent of the gross receipts.

After the initial excitement of having the Bill passed through Parliament, progress was slow and there also seemed to be a lack of interest from the LBSCR. The contactor, William Hudson also left the B&DR and was replaced by Henry Jackson. On July 18th 1881 under a new chairman, the Hon. Ashley Ponsonby, the promoters obtained a second Act which extended the time for the completion of the line to August 2nd 1885. Under Henry Jackson, the engineer was Alex L. Nimmo, but he was soon to give way to Charles O. Blaber who had been one of the proposed engineers for most of the original schemes and was fast becoming well known in his profession. The acting engineer to Henry Jackson was G. Waller Willocks of Westminster.

The ceremony of turning the first sod took place on June 2nd 1883, just south west of the Dyke Hotel and was performed by Mrs. Davey, the wife of Alderman Davey, JP. After the ceremony, lunch was served in a marquee.

Problems soon set in for the B&DR and a new board of directors were appointed, although the Hon. Ashley Ponsonby remained as chairman. The company address was given as 20 Budge Row, Cannon Street, London E.C. The appointed company solicitor was J.Leslie Powell of 17, Essex Street, Strand, London W.C.

With hard chalk causing construction difficulties towards the Dyke, it soon became clear that the B&DR would be unable to complete the line by August 2nd 1885, as required by the July 18th 1881 Act, and they were able to obtain powers for a deviation towards the terminus. At this time it would seem that the new railway was still being considered as two separate lines, as the deviation was described as follows:-

A railway commencing in the parish of Hangleton by a junction with the authorised Brighton and Dyke Railway now in course of construction, at a point 15 chains or thereabouts in a north-westerly direction from the building or shed known as "Skeleton Hovel", and terminating in the parish of Poynings at a point 2 chains or thereabouts in a south-easterly direction from the cow house adjacent to the Dyke Cottages on Poynings Place Farm.

Further applications for extensions were made to Parliament, which resulted in first an Act of June 4th 1886, giving a deadline of June 1st 1887 followed by an Act of August 8th 1887, giving a deadline of September 1st 1887. By then, the new railway was considered as one line, without a junction at Hangleton.

The Tuesday, August 30th 1887 edition of the *Sussex Daily News* reported that the new line was inspected on the previous day by Major General Hutchinson of the Board of Trade. The *Sussex Daily News* went on to report :-

The new railway joins the Brighton and Portsmouth line of the London, Brighton and South Coast Railway at a point about half a mile from West Brighton Station and is about three miles and a half in length, the terminus being situated three or four hundred yards from the Dyke Hotel. The soil is of a hard, chalky formation all the way, so hard that it had to be blasted with power. At present there is only a single line, though the bridges have been built to allow for a double line. The construction of the permanent way is similar to that of the London, Brighton and South Coast Railway Company, 84 lb. steel rails being laid, with 40 lb chairs, and with spikes and trenails on vertical sleepers creosoted, which are placed on a foundation of chalk ballast and a top ballast of gravel from Chichester. The railway rises from the junction at a gradient of 1 in 40 until it reaches the terminus, which is 700 feet above the level of the sea.

The report continued:-

The bridges that are beneath the line were tested by Major General Hutchinson with one of the Brighton Company's steam engines, and they did not deflect a sixteenth of an inch. No tunnelling has been necessary, but there are several deep cuttings, one of them, where the railway crosses the Hangleton Farm, being as much as 40 ft deep. A station has been erected at the Dyke Terminus, but as yet it is not completed in every respect. The platform, for at present there is only one, though plenty of room is left for a second when the necessity arises, is three hundred feet in length by fifteen feet broad, and is built of brick and coping. The building, comprising three rooms, about 15 ft square a ticket office, general waiting room, and 'ladies' waiting room is constructed of galvanised iron and match-boarded inside. The station-master's house is not yet built, nor is the goods yard finished. It is proposed to build a station at Hangleton, and there is an idea of extending the line through Poynings to Henfield, where it would form a junction with the Horsham line. But these things are yet without form and reach will probably depend upon the working of the line that has been completed as to whether they are carried into existence. With regard to the position of the Brighton and Dyke Railway Company they have entered into an agreement with the London, Brighton and South Coast Railway Company by which the latter undertake to work the line for 55 per cent. of the receipts handing over the other 45 per cent. to the shareholders of the new Company. In addition to this, the London, Brighton and South Coast Railway guarantee 4 per cent. on the debentures. A saloon carriage was hooked on to the 9.30 train from London Bridge yesterday morning for the accommodation of the Inspector and the officials of the Railway Companies who accompanied him. At Preston Park the carriage was unhooked, a special train formed and the party proceeded direct to West Brighton and then on the new line. Accompanying Major General Hutchinson were Mr. Banister (Chief Engineer of the L.B. and S.C. Railway), Mr.J.Richard's (Traffic Superintendent), Mr.E.Houghton (Telegraph Superintendent), Mr.Perry (Superintendent of the Permanent Way), Mr.W.Smith (Chief Permanent Way Inspector, Brighton District), Mr.Fossey (Permanent Way Inspector, Brighton District), Mr.Page (Traffic Inspector, Brighton District), Mr.Waller representative of Messrs. Saxby and Farmer who supply the signalling apparatus, Mr.J.L.Powell (Solicitor to the Brighton and Dyke Railway Company), Mr.C.O.Blaber (Engineer to the Brighton and Dyke Railway Company), and Mr.H.Jackson (Contractor). On his arrival at the Dyke, after careful inspection, Major General Hutchinson expressed satisfaction at the way in which the work had been done and said that the railway was in a fit state to be opened for traffic. Lunch was then partaken of at the Dyke Station and the party returned to town by the 3.48 train. The line will be formally opened by the Chairman of the Company, the Hon. Ashley Ponsonby, on Thursday, September 1st, at half past twelve o'clock, when a luncheon will be held at the Dyke while a regular service of trains, it is understood, will commence to run as early as eight o'clock on that morning. As far as the present arrangements go it seems that there will be ten trains each way in the course of the day, run at intervals of about an hour.

As mentioned in this report, the line did in fact open on Thursday, September 1st 1887, and although the ceremonial train which was pulled by E class 0-6-0T called *Orleans*, designed by William Stroadley (the LBSCR Locomotive Superintendent from 1870 to 1890) left Brighton Station at 12 noon, it was not the first train to travel over the line, as trains on the first day were running strictly to the timetable (as also mentioned in the report) and this honour fell to a Stroadley designed "Terrier" A class 0-6-0T called *Piccadilly* which left Brighton at 8.00 a.m. and arrived at the Dyke

LONDON BRIGHTON & SOUTH COAST RAILWAY.

OPENING

OF THE

BRIGHTON & DYKE RAILWAY

SEPTEMBER, 1887.

On and from Thursday, September 1st, 1887, the above Railway will be opened for

PASSENGER TRAFFIC

And Trains will be run between BRIGHTON (Central Station), WEST BRIGHTON and THE DYKE, as under:—

DOWN.	WEEK DAYS.								SUNDAYS.				
	a.m.	a.m.	a.m	noon.	p.m.	p.m.	p.m.	p.m.	a.m	a.m.	p.m.	p.m.	p.m.
BRIGHTON (Central) ... dep.	8 0	9 15	10 35	12 0	1 25	2 50	4 15	5 40	9 35	11 15	2 40	3 40	5 25
West Brighton ... ... „	8 5	9 20	10 40	12 5	1 30	2 55	4 20	5 45	9 40	11 20	2 45	3 45	5 30
THE DYKE ... ... arr.	8 20	9 35	10 55	12 20	1 45	3 10	4 35	6 0	9 55	11 35	3 0	4 0	5 45

UP.	WEEK DAYS.								SUNDAYS.				
	a.m.	a.m.	a.m.	p.m.	p.m.	p.m.	p.m.	p.m.	a.m.	noon.	p.m.	p.m.	p.m.
THE DYKE ... ... dep.	8 45	9 55	11 20	12 35	2 0	3 25	5 0	6 30	10 25	12 0	3 10	4 30	6 20
West Brighton ... ... „	8 58	10 8	11 33	12 48	2 13	3 38	5 13	6 43	10 38	12 13	3 23	4 43	6 33
BRIGHTON (Central) arr.	9 5	10 15	11 40	12 55	2 20	3 45	5 20	6 50	10 45	12 20	3 30	4 50	6 40

All Trains First, Second and Third Class.

FARES BETWEEN BRIGHTON (Central Station) OR WEST BRIGHTON AND THE DYKE	SINGLE.						RETURN.					
	First Class.		Second Class.		Third Class.		First Class.		Second Class.		Third Class.	
	s.	d.	s.	d.	s.	d.	s.	d.	s.	d.	s.	d.
	1	0	0	9	0	5	1	6	1	2	0	10

London Bridge Terminus,
August 30th, 1887.

(By Order) A. SARLE, Secretary and General Manager.

(2,000—30.8.87.)

Waterlow & Sons Limited, Printers, London Wall, London.

A handbill advertising the opening of the new railway.

Author's Collection

Station with a saloon, a first class and four third class carriages as well as a guards van. Carrying about thirty passengers, which included the contractor Henry Jackson, the train also brought various items for the terminus, which included a clock, bell, seats and tables. The formal opening was fully covered by the *Sussex Daily News* in their Friday, September 2nd 1887 edition as follows:-

THE BRIGHTON AND DYKE RAILWAY
OPENING CEREMONY AND LUNCHEON

There was very little of ceremony or of incident at the formal opening, yesterday, of the new Brighton and Dyke Railway. At twelve noon a special train, the engine of which was gaily bedecked with bunting and miniature flags, left Brighton Central Station for the purpose of conveying along the new line those of its promoters who were able to attend, a good many shareholders, and several representatives of the Press. West Brighton was reached at 12.5, and then the journey to the unpretentious little station high up on the Southdowns was made without further stoppage. On arrival at the Dyke, the party detrained, and gathered on the platform, around the Hon. Ashley Ponsonby, the Chairman of the Brighton and Dyke Railway, who, without making a speech, simply declared the new line open for public traffic. Three cheers were called for and given, and "one cheer more" for the Hon. Mrs. Ponsonby, who was presented by Miss Jackson with an enormous and very beautiful bouquet, composed almost entirely of orchids and other rare exotic flowers. Rain now began to fall - indeed, it scarcely ceased throughout the afternoon, greatly militating against everyone's pleasure while out of doors; and so an immediate move was made for the large tent which had been erected on a rather sharp incline of the Downs a little to the west of the station. Here, at two o'clock, luncheon was served in very admirable style by Mr.E.Booth, of East-street, Brighton. The floral decorations of the tables were much admired, the flowers being arranged so as to make the presentation of a bouquet to each of the ladies present - a pleasant and convenient ceremony at the conclusion of the repast. The Hon. Ashley Ponsonby occupied the chair. The vice-chair was taken by Mr. John Saxby. On the immediate right of the Chairman sat Mrs. Gabrielli, Mr. Banister (chief engineer of the L.B. and S.C. Railway), and Mrs.Powell; and on his immediate left Mrs.Jackson (wife of the contractor of the new line), Major Jarvis, and the Hon. Mrs.Ponsonby. The Mayor of Brighton (Alderman E.J.Reeves), who sat at the upper table, had on his right the Mayoress (Mrs.Reeves) and on his left Mrs.Davey, wife of Alderman Davey.

It is interesting to note that in this report the *Sussex Daily News* mentioned that the line was declared open by the Chairman the Hon. Ashley Ponsonby without making a speech, while the *Brighton Hearld* reported in their issue of September 3rd 1887, that Mrs. Ashley Ponsonby declared the line open, also without making a speech. In view of both these statements and how long ago they were written, it is unclear who actually did perform this duty, although the report in the *Sussex Daily News* does give far more detail of the days proceedings.

The *Sussex Daily News* went on to say that amongst the many other guests were Mr.W.Stroadley (Chief of the Locomotive Department of the LBSCR), Mr.C.O.Blaber (Engineer to the Brighton and Dyke Railway) and his wife, Mr.R.L.Cripps (Estate agent of the LBSCR) plus members of the Council and their wifes. The report also rather quaintly mentioned the following:-

Several other persons, some of whom occupy subordinate positions in the service of the London, Brighton, and South Coast Railway Company and the Brighton and Dyke Railway Company, also sat down. During the luncheon and between the toasts, the band of the 1st Volunteer (Sussex) Brigade Cinque Ports Division Royal Artillery, under the conductorship of Mr.W.Davis, enchanted everyone's enjoyment by the performance of a delightful selection of music.

Following the luncheon, the usual loyal toasts were given and someone called for three cheers for the Queen; and these were given with great heartiness, the band then played the National Anthem. The band also, after the toast of the Heir Apparent had been honoured, performed, in brilliant style, "God bless the Prince of Wales".

Many of the speeches made reference to the Devil himself, and these ranged from "the dark and dangerous enemy of man" to a certain "old gentleman", who had happily been driven away before the completion of his full purpose. In fact, so many speeches mentioned the original "engineer" of the Dyke that the proposer of the toast of "The Ladies" was tempted into bluntly protesting that it was about time they "let the Devil go to the Devil".

During his speech Mr.F.Banister mentioned that the LBSCR would do all they could to help the B&DR and said that his only regret was that Mr.Jackson had not carried the railway still "higher up" to the summit. He went on to humorously suggest a change of name for the locality. For instance, what would people think of an address such as say "William Hall, Esq., Paradise, Devil's Dyke". Mr. William Stroudley followed Mr. Banister and although he thought Mr. Jackson had done his work well, he echoed Mr. Banister's regret that the line had not been taken to the top of the hill. This last statement was met with tokens of decided approval by those present; and several voices cried out "so it will; so it will!".

After the line was opened it was considered to be a great success, and on the first Sunday of operation, the issue of tickets had to be suspended as it was soon realised that the Sunday service was insufficient and special trains had to be arranged. With all this happening, there were soon rumours of a station at Hangleton and also the line being extended to Henfield. As time moved on and with the initial interest falling away, these rumours were soon forgotten.

With the new branch from Brighton to the Dyke now up and running, it was thought that other attractions at the summit would be a good idea, and in 1892 the Dyke Hotel and Estate was bought by James Henry Hubbard who built up the facilities to such an extent that on Whit Monday 1893, it was reported that some 30,000 people visited the Estate, which by now included many amusements and sideshows. On Sundays, visitors could even listen to the Dyke Park Estate Brass and Reed Band. Mr. Hubbard even published his own "Devil's Dyke Times" with an estimated circulation of one million. Whether this optimistic circulation was ever reached is not known, but it is thought that it was published at least on four occasions, and consisted of 16 pages, costing 1d per copy.

An early view of the Dyke Station with a set of six 4-wheeled carriages soon after the line had opened. Note how the platform had yet to be extended to incorporate the signal box and the later built goods siding.
Author's Collection

E3 class 0-6-2T No.168 arriving with the branch train at the Dyke Station. Lens of Sutton

An unidentified train approaching the station. Note the former carriage (on the left of the photograph) which was used as a refreshment room in the early days. Lens of Sutton

This view of the station shows the goods yard after it was completed. Lens of Sutton

At about this time, with the backing of Mr. Hubbard, a civil engineer named William Brewer came up with three ideas, as added transport attractions at the Dyke. The first was for a light cable tramway from the existing Dyke Station to the Dyke Hotel and Estate. The second was for an aerial cableway flight across the ravine, and the third idea was for a type of steep grade railway on the north side of Dyke Hill.

Nothing came of the first proposal, but the aerial cableway across the ravine was built and opened on October 13th 1894, while the steep grade railway was also built and opened on July 24th 1897.

The aerial cableway was quite revolutionary at that time, but was probably considered more of an added attraction to the Dyke Hotel and Estate than of great means of transport, although the possibilities of this means of crossing a large expanse elsewhere was great. The promoters were Telpher Cable and Cliff Railway Syndicate Limited, and the cableway was constructed in 1894 by Cable Tramways Construction and Conversion Company Limited at a cost of £5,000. The opening ceremony on October 13th 1894 was performed by the Mayor of Brighton, Mr. W. Botting after he and the Mayoress, together with Mr. William T. Spink, the Chairman of Telpher Cable and Cliff Railway Syndicate Limited, and Mr. William Brewer, had crossed the ravine in the official inaugural car and returned.

The aerial cableway whicn crossed the ravine. Note the cable-car which is halfway across. The inset shows the entrance to the Dyke Hotel (in the background) and Park Estate. R.C.Riley Collection

The steep grade railway was built in 1897 and had a definite transport function. It connected the Dyke with the picturesque village of Poynings, which although only about a mile away, lay some 480 ft below the Downs. The land was leased to Pyamidical Syndicate Ltd. of London by Mr. Hubbard, at a ground rent of £100 per annum, while the line was to be owned and operated as the Brighton Dyke Steep Grade Railway Ltd. and was constructed by Courtney & Birkett of Southwick, who were a yacht building firm. The engineer was Mr. Charles O. Blaber who (as previously mentioned) was also the engineer to the standard gauge Brighton & Dyke Railway. The line consisted of two 3 ft gauge lines, 840 ft in length of differing gradients. The two cars which seated 14 passengers, were supplied by Ashbury Railway Carriage & Iron Company and were opened sided, although they had roofs.

Two views of the steep grade railway. R.C.Riley Collection

The steep grade railway was opened on July 24th 1897 by Sir Henry Howarth M.P. at the top station in the presence of a large gathering.

For a pleasant day out, it was now possible to travel from Brighton by train to the Dyke Station, cross the ravine by the aerial cableway and descend down to Poynings for a cream tea, via the steep grade railway, and as an added bonus for anyone who enjoyed travelling on railways there was even a small Switchback Railway as part of the fairground attractions at the Dyke Hotel & Estate.

With Mr. Hubbard running into financial difficulties and eventually emigrating to Canada in 1909, the aerial cableway and the steep grade railway had lost their main supporter and coincidentally suffered declining numbers of passengers. Both seemed to have closed by 1909 although the exact dates are uncertain.

Even before the building and demise of the aerial cableway and the steep grade railway, the original railway from Brighton to the Dyke seems to have had its problems, with the decreasing number of passengers. In 1891 a private halt was provided for the benefit of Brighton and Hove Golf Club, which had opened in October 1887. This halt consisted of a long brick built platform and a nameboard and was situated 62 chains from the Dyke Station, approximately 50 yards from the Golf Club House.

An agreement between the Railway Company and the Golf Club came into being on January 9th 1895, when a electric bell was installed in the Golf Club House which would ring when the starting signal was lowered at the Dyke Station and continue until the signal was replaced.

Despite the opening of the Golf Club Halt, the financial problems of the B&DR continued and the very future of the line looked uncertain. On November 18th 1895, Mr. John F.R.Daniel was appointed Receiver by an Order dated November 1895. Mr. Daniel was no stranger to the perils of running an independent railway as he was Managing Director of the Weston, Clevedon & Portishead Railway in Somerset. In fact the B&DR was to continue in Receivership until it was absorbed (like the LBSCR) into the Southern Railway after the 1923 grouping.

After the goods siding at the terminus was completed and passed inspection by Major General Hutchinson in 1892, the first train of the day was a mixed passenger and goods train. The main goods received was coal, coke and cattle food while baled straw and trussed hay was sent out. Parcels received were normally for the Dyke Hotel, Golf Club or the villages of Fulking or Poynings. The delivery of these parcels was usually by a local coal merchant who received one penny for each one delivered.

The goods siding just after it was opened. Lens of Sutton

On September 3rd 1905 a halt was opened on the main Brighton - Portsmouth line, near the branch junction and was appropriately called Dyke Junction Halt. As this new halt was situated on the Brighton side of the junction signal box, it was of great value to the Dyke branch. Like several other similar halts the LBSCR had opened at about the same time, it consisted of two wooden platforms. The main reason that these halts were being introduced was to answer the competition of street tramcars. They soon became known as "Motor Halts" or "Rail Motor Halts" as the LBSCR were at that time using single pull-and-push carriages with "Terrier" 0-6-0T's. Because of the balloon shape of these carriages, they not so surprisingly, soon became known as "Balloons". Dyke Junction Halt was renamed Aldrington Halt on June 17th 1932.

As an economy measure, like many similar country branch lines, the line to the Dyke was closed completely during the First World War from January 1st 1917 and reopened on July 26th 1920.

After the war, the line returned to normal service and was even used for one or two railway experiments, including the Angus Train Control System, which as the very title suggests, was a system devised by Mr.A.R.Angus, an Australian, for controlling train movements which involved sending an engine into a section occupied by another engine. When this happened, steam was automatically shut off and the brakes applied. Two "Terrier" 0-6-0T's were hired from the LBSCR for these tests, they were No.643 formerly called *Gipsyhill* and No.680 formerly called *Bookham*, and were fitted with a device which supplied a low voltage alternating current to the track, so long as the section was clear. When another train was already in this section, the train was brought to a stop, even though the driver did not have to touch the controls. Although these trials were apparently successful, the system was later dismantled.

As we have already read, like the LBSCR, the B&DR became part of the newly formed Southern Railway after the 1923 grouping, and although things remained very much as they had before, eventually the goods traffic was considered insufficient enough to retain the goods siding at the terminus and was withdrawn from January 2nd 1933.

One interesting idea for the branch that the Southern Railway did try out was a Sentinel steam railbus in 1933. Built in 1932 by the Sentinel Wagon Works at Shrewsbury, and sent to the Metropolitan Cammell Company in Birmingham to have the body fitted, it had trials over the line, and after various adjustments, the Sentinel steam railbus entered into public service on the Dyke line on May 1st 1933.

Two views of the Sentinel steam railbus at the Dyke Station on October 11th 1933.

The late H.C.Casserley

On December 18th 1933 a new halt was opened on the line, just a half mile from the junction and known as Rowan Halt. It was built to serve the developing area which included the Aldrington Manor Estate, north of the Old Shoreham Road. The official opening of the halt was not until January 12th 1934 and the Saturday January 13th 1934 edition of the *Sussex Daily News* reported this special event as follows:-

ROWAN HALT

HOVE'S NEW RAILWAY STATION

OFFICIAL OPENING

Building enterprise and railway enterprise joined hands yesterday in an interesting ceremony at Hove. The event was the official opening of the Rowan Halt on the Dyke branch line, which has been provided by the Southern Railway to meet the needs of the Aldrington Manor Estate, the creation of Braybons, Ltd.

The Estate, situated to the north of the Old Shoreham-road, will comprise 360 houses of attractive design, providing the most modern and convenient accommodation. Some 250 have been completed, and they are sold as fast as Messrs. Braybon can build them. The situation of the estate is a very healthy and pleasant one, and the recreation ground which it is intended to form will be a still further addition to its amenities. With the opening of the Rowan Halt, nothing is lacking in the way of transport facilities, and a pathway and bridge over the line give quick access to Old Shoreham-road.

To attend the opening ceremony a small party gathered at noon at Hove Town Hall and drove to the railway station, where they joined one of the comfortable rail-buses that now serve the Dyke line. A stroke of humour was provided by the motor hooter which had been attached to the car and which effectively heralded the arrival at the halt of its distinguished passengers, who included the Mayor and Mayoress of Hove (Councillor Victor R. Hudson J.P., and Mrs. Hudson), Mr.T.R.Braybon, Mr.Ernest Davis and Councillor Lewis C. Cohen (Directors of Braybons Ltd), and Mr.C.Graseman (Public Relations Officer of the Southern Railway).

Mr.Davis first introduced Mr.Graseman, who, on behalf of the Southern Railway, asked the Mayor to declare the halt open. He hoped it would soon become a large station.

The Mayor, in declaring the halt open, said the development of the borough was exceedingly gratifying to him, and the manner in which that part of the town had grown was really wonderful. The necessity for the halt had arisen solely out of the enterprise of Messrs. Braybon in developing the Aldrington Manor Estate, and he was happy to acknowledge on behalf of the Town Council the credit due to the firm. The halt was also proof of the foresight of the Southern Railway.

After a tour of the estate the party drove to the First-avenue Hotel, where luncheon - in every way worthy of the hotel - was served with Mr. Ernest Davis in the chair.

The official opening of Rowan Halt on January 12th 1934, after the Sentinel steam railbus (inset) had arrived from Hove. The Sussex Daily News

To mark his retirement, a surprise presentation of pipes and tobacco was made by local school children to Guard Wright at Rowan Halt on January 21st 1938. Southern Railway Magazine

As the 1930's moved on, it became obvious that the railway to the Dyke was nearing the end of its life. The summer saw many full trains climbing up the slopes of the South Downs but the winter trains would often run without any passengers, while about half of the winter service terminated at Rowan Halt. The full run to the Dyke now had competition from the Southdown Bus Company, who were able to offer passengers a quicker ride to the Dyke Hotel without having to walk the 200 ft climb from the Dyke Station. The line closed on December 31st 1938.

D3 class 0-4-4T No.377 with a single carriage at the Dyke Station. Lens of Sutton

Description of the Route

The scenery between Brighton and the Dyke was contrasting. Trains would leave Brighton Station in very suburban surroundings and continue in a westerly direction along the main line, through Holland Road Halt (opened on September 3rd 1905), and then Hove Station (originally opened as Cliftonville in 1865 and then West Brighton in 1879, later changing to Hove and West Brighton in 1894, and finally Hove in 1895), before heading off north at Dyke Junction, and climbing the vast open spaces of the South Downs towards the Dyke Station.

The Sentinel steam railbus being prepared at Brighton Station for the next trip to the Dyke.
The National Railway Museum

E4 class 0-6-2T No.2566 leaving Brighton Station with the branch train to the Dyke on June 25th 1938.
R.F.Roberts

The Sentinel steam railbus stops at Hove Station on the way to the Dyke. October 11th 1933.
The late H.C.Casserley

Continuing on the main line from Hove, trains would pass through Aldrington Halt, which was situated just before reaching the junction. Opened as Dyke Junction Halt on September 3rd 1905, it originally consisted of two wooden platforms, and at one time, a loop siding into the Hove Electric Light Works, which was on the 'up' side of the main line. It was re-named Aldrington Halt on June 17th 1932 and it is interesting to note that some old local maps of the area indicate that the halt was very slightly moved from its original position near to the junction, to its current position.

Terrier 0-6-0T No.79 *Minories* with a "balloon" shaped trailer carriage forming a 'motor train' for Worthing at Dyke Junction Halt. J.Scott-Morgan Collection

The Sentinel steam railbus stops at Aldrington Halt on the way back to Brighton from the Dyke. October 11th 1933 The late H.C.Casserley

Terrier 0-6-0T No.79 *Minories* returns from Worthing with the single trailer 'motor train' and passes the junction with the Dyke branch (right of photograph). Author's Collection

Having left the main line at the junction where the signal box had a 21 lever frame, the single track branch curved away towards Hangleton and passed under an iron girder bridge by which the Old Shoreham Road crossed over the line. At about this point, the line started to climb a gradient of 1 in 40 for the next 3 miles.

Just a half mile from the junction, Rowan Halt, which had opened on December 18th 1933 was situated on the 'up' side of the line. Built to serve the local developing area and officially opened on January 12th 1934, it consisted of a 70 ft long wooden platform with a corrugated iron shelter and a iron footbridge.

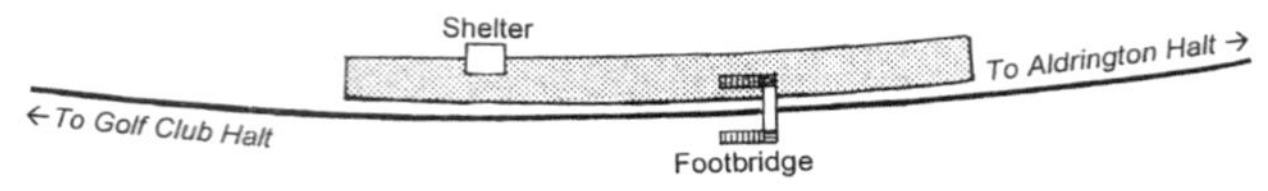

ROWAN HALT

This view of the branch train was taken from 22 Rowan Avenue in 1936.

E.Mason / G.Dinnage Collection. Courtesy of Margaret Stevenson

From here the line passed over Hangleton Road by a plate girder bridge, and also over what is now West Way, by a brick arch bridge and continued a 1 in 40 climb through a 40 ft deep cutting and under a brick arch bridge, and then on its way up the South Downs.

The Hangleton Road Bridge (left) and a general view of the climb up the South Downs (right).

Author's Collection

E4 class 0-6-2T No.2566 returning with the branch train down the 1 in 40 gradient on the way back to Brighton. G.A.Strickler

Just 62 chains short of the terminus, the Golf Club Halt was reached, which consisted of a single brick platform situated on the 'up' side of the line. The halt never appeared in any timetable and was only really used by members of the Brighton & Hove Golf Club, who had to book through to the Dyke as no tickets were issued bearing the title of Golf Club Halt or Golf Club Platform, as the nameboard on the platform read.

←To Dyke

GOLF CLUB HALT

To Rowan Halt→

The platform at Golf Club Halt in 1939. A.E.Bissell / G.Dinnage Collection

The summit of the branch in 1939.
A.E.Bissell / G.Dinnage Collection

Double header at the Dyke Station on April 13th 1933.
A.E.Bissell / G.Dinnage Collection

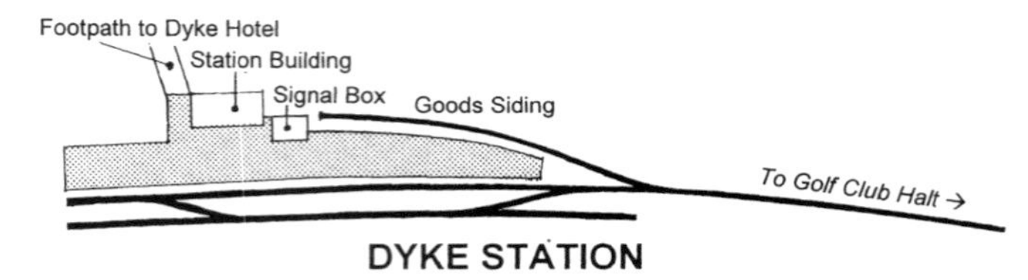

When opened, the Dyke Station consisted of a single 300 ft brick faced platform, a passing loop, a single storey corrugated iron station building which comprised of a ticket office, a general waiting room and a ladies waiting room, and was similar in appearance to the type of station buildings that Col. Stephens used on some of the lines which he was involved with, notably the Hawkhurst branch and the Rye & Camber Tramway. Next to the station building was the footpath which led towards the Dyke Hotel and the other attractions. On the other side of the footpath, and to the back of the platform, was at one time, a former railway carriage which was used as a refreshment room, although during the Southern Railway period, this was later removed.

The original signalling equipment supplied by Saxby and Farmer were slotted post signals but these were soon replaced by standard lower quadrants. When the station was opened, the 15 lever signal box stood on its own next to the platform, but when the platform was extended, it incorporated not only the signal box, but also served the single track goods siding which ran towards the back of the station and was completed in 1892.

One very unusual feature at this particular terminus was the absence of any buffer stops at the very end of the line. Surprisingly, they were considered unnecessary because the line finished just short of a chalk face.

Gradient Profile

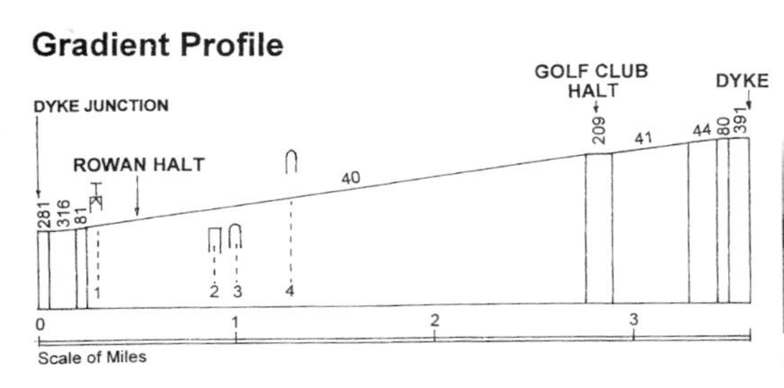

Approaching the Dyke Station.
R.C.Riley Collection

The end of the line at the Dyke Station in 1938. Note the absence of any buffer stops apart from the siding (right).
A.E.Bissell / G.Dinnage Collection

A general view of the station.
The late Dr.I.C.Allen. Courtsey of R.C.Riley

Motive Power and Rolling Stock

With William Stroadley becoming the LBSCR Locomotive Superintendent in 1870, it is not such a surprise that the ceremonial train was pulled by one of his E class 0-6-0T locomotives which was called "Orleans", while the very first train over the line was pulled by one of his "Terrier" A class 0-6-0T locomotives called *Piccadilly.*

Although "Terriers" were used in the early days, as the line settled down, the usual locomotives were either the E4 class 0-6-2T's designed by R.J.Billinton (the LBSCR Locomotive Superintendent from 1890 to 1905) or Stroadley D1 class 0-4-2T's, while the passenger trains normally consisted of two to four 4-wheeled carriages and later two or three 8-wheeled carriages. In 1905 the LBSCR obtained two steam railcars from Beyer, Peacock and Co., and these were not so surprisingly known as No.1 and No.2. The latter was tried on the branch and although it was quite satisfactory when the winter time traffic was sparse, it was considered totally inadequate during the holiday season. At about the same time, one of the two petrol railcars which the LBSCR had obtained from Dick, Kerr and Co. and known as No.3 and No.4 following on in sequence from the two steam railways, was also tried on the branch, but in the words of J.N.Maskelyne writing in the February 1932 issue of *The Model Railway News,* they were "anything but man enough for the job".

When the Dyke Junction Halt was opened in 1905 to deal with the 'motor -trains' on the main Brighton-Portsmouth line (which normally consisted of a "Terrier" 0-6-0T and a single pull-and-push "balloon" shaped carriage), these 'motor-trains' were even tried briefly on the branch. As the "balloon" shaped carriages did not have a hand-brake, it was naturally considered unsafe on such a steep line and the 'motor-trains' were soon withdrawn. From then on, all locomotives would lead and on reaching the Dyke Station, they would run round and would be first on descending. Often a single locomotive and a "balloon" carriage would give the impression that it was a 'motor-train' when, in fact, it was not.

E1 class 0-6-0T No.159 with a "balloon" shaped carriage at the Dyke Station. Lens of Sutton

I3 class 4-4-2T No.2089 having just arrived with the branch train at the Dyke Station. Lens of Sutton

Other locomotives which were known to have worked on the line were Stroadley E1 class 0-6-0T's, Billinton E3 class 0-6-2T's, E5 class 0-6-2T's, D3 class 0-4-4T's, plus the I2 and I3 class 4-4-2T's designed by D.Earle Marsh (the LBSCR Locomotive Superintendent from 1905 to 1911), and I1X class 4-4-2T's designed be R.E.L. Maunsell (the Southern Railway Chief Mechanical Engineer from 1923 to 1937). Some tender locomotives were also noted on the line, ranging from Billinton C2 class 0-6-0's to Marsh C2X class 0-6-0's.

As also previously mentioned, the line became well known to railway observers for its use of the Sentinel steam railbus. Built during 1932 to the requirements of R.E.L.Maunsell and completed by January 1933 at the Sentinel Wagon Works at Shrewsbury, it was then sent to the Metropolitan Cammell Company in Birmingham to have the body fitted, and came into service on the branch on May 1st 1933 after various trial runs on the line, and in the Brighton area. Contrary to some reports, despite several problems during its early days, the Sentinel steam railbus was quite popular with the public, and after Rowan Halt had opened it was even more so. Unfortunately, it could not handle a large amount of passengers during a busy period and on some occasions had to give way to a conventional locomotive and two carriages.

The steam railbus remained in service on the Dyke branch until May 1st 1935, when after having a fractured bogie bolster repaired, it never returned and was moved on to the Westerham branch in Kent. After laying idle behind the Tonbridge engine shed, it was scrapped at Ashford works in the mid to late 1940's.

Sentinel steam railbus approaching the Dyke Station. National Railway Museum

I1X class 4-4-2T No.2602 with the branch train at the Dyke Station in the mid 1930's. Lens of Sutton

E5 class 0-6-2T No.B586 waits at the Dyke Station in the late 1920's.. Lens of Sutton

Operation

When the line was first opened, the train staff and ticket system was used. The staff stations were Hove and the Dyke, while the ticket colour was red. From October 6th 1920 the LBSCR changed this system to Webb and Thompson's electric train staff, which was exchanged at the junction.

LBSCR Appendix. June 1917

SPECIAL INSTRUCTIONS RESPECTING CERTAIN PLACES - *continued*

Dyke Railway. - No engines must work on the Dyke Railway unless it is fitted with the Westinghouse Brake, and this must be in thorough working order. The Driver must ascertain, by personal inspection, that the taps on the connections between each carriage are open with the main pipe, and he must not start with a Train if any of the Brakes are shut off. The Train must not be started from Hove, or the Dyke Station, until the Guard has tested the Brake by putting it full on, by opening the cock on the rear vehicle; the Driver will be held personally responsible that this is done on every occasion before starting the Train from either of these Stations.

A Platform at the Golf Club House is in use for Passengers to join, or leave Trains, but the Station Masters at Brighton, Hove, and the Dyke, as well as the Guards, must take care that no Train, unless it is carrying the Train Staff, is stopped at this Platform, either to take up or set down Passengers.

When Trains are carrying the Train Staff, Drivers and Guards running from Dyke to Brighton must always keep a good look-out for Passengers standing on the Platform, and arrange to stop thereat to take them up.

When Ordinary Trains are employed to work the Service on the Dyke Railway in place of the Motor Cars, Special Carriages must be locked up by the Conductor before starting, for Passengers to and from the Halts, and the Driver must also be advised before starting what part of the Train is to be stopped alongside the Platform at the Halts.

E4 class 0-6-2T No.2494 prepares to head south from the Dyke Station with a single carriage.
Lens of Sutton

Timetables and Tickets

JULY 1922

BRIGHTON and THE DYKE (Motor Cars—3rd class only).—London, Brighton, and South Coast.

Miles	Down.	Week Days. d	mrn		aft	aft		aft	aft		aft		Sundays. mrn		mrn		aft		aft		
—	Brighton (Central) ¶ ..dep.	10 5	11 15	....	12 30	1 40	....	2 30	3 48	....	4 57	....	10 5	....	1130	....	2 30	....	5 0	....	....
1½	Hove ¶	1014	11 20	....	12 35	1 45	....	2 35	3 53	....	5 2	....	1010	....	1135	....	2 35	....	5 5	....	....
5½	The Dyke..............arr.	1031	11 36	....	12 41	....	....	2 51	4 9	....	5 18	....	1026	....	1151	....	2 51	....	5 21	....	....

Miles	Up.	Week Days. d		mrn	aft		aft	aft		aft	aft			Sundays. mrn		aft		aft		aft		
—	The Dyke ¶ ....dep.	1055	....	1157	1 0	....	....	3 5	....	4 20	5 42	....	....	11 0	....	1230	....	4 20	....	5 30	....	....
4	Hove ¶	1113	....	1211	1 14	....	1 58	3 19	....	4 34	5 56	....	....	1113	....	1243	....	4 33	....	5 43	....	....
5½	Brighton (Central) ....arr.	1118	....	1218	1 21	....	2 3	3 26	....	4 41	6 3	....	....	1120	....	1250	....	4 40	....	5 50	....	....

d Does not stop at the Halts.

¶ "Halts" at Holland Road, between Brighton and Hove: and Dyke Junction, between Hove and The Dyke.

JULY 1938

BRIGHTON and THE DYKE (one class only)

Down — Week Days (mrn … aft)

Miles	HOUR	6	7	7	8	9	10	11	12	12	2	3	4	5	6	S 7	E 7	8
—	Brighton ....dep	42	14	42	13	10	10	.	8	42	10	10	10	7	10	7	10	8
1	Holland Road Halt..	44	.	44	.	12	12	.	10	44	12	12	12	9	12	9	12	10
1¼	Hove................	46	17	46	16	14	14	12	12	46	14	14	14	11	14	11	14	12
2	Aldrington Halt.....	48	.	48	19	16	16	14	14	48	16	16	16	13	16	13	16	14
2¼	Rowan Halt G.......	52	21	52	23	19	19	17	18	51	19	19	19	16	19	16	19	17
5¼	The Dyke.......arr.	.	.	.	.	30	30	28	.	2	30	30	30	27	30	27	30	28

Down — Sundays (mrn … aft)

Miles	HOUR	10	11	12	1	2	3	4	5	6	7	8
—	Brighton ....dep	10	10	8	.	10	10	10	10	10	8	10
1	Holland Road Halt..	13	12	10	.	13	12	12	13	12	10	.
1¼	Hove................	15	14	12	12	15	14	14	15	14	12	15
2	Aldrington Halt.....	17	16	14	13	17	16	16	17	16	14	16
2¼	Rowan Halt G.......	20	19	17	16	20	19	19	20	19	17	19
5¼	The Dyke.......arr.	31	30	28	27	31	30	30	31	30	28	30

Up — Week Days (mrn … aft)

Miles	HOUR	7	7	8	8	9	10	11	12	1	2	3	4	5	6	7	8
—	The Dyke.......dep.	.	.	.	.	37	37	37	.	20	37	37	39	37	37	37	37
3	Rowan Halt G.......	0	24	0	33	46	46	46	29	29	46	46	48	47	47	47	47
3¼	Aldrington Halt.....	2	26	2	35	49	49	49	31	32	49	49	51	50	50	50	50
4	Hove................	4	28	4	37	51	51	51	33	34	51	51	54	52	52	52	52
4½	Holland Road Halt..	6	30	7	40	53	53	53	36	36	53	53	56	54	54	54	54
5¼	Brighton ....arr.	10	34	10	44	57	57	57	39	40	57	57	0	58	58	58	58

Up — Sundays (mrn … aft)

Miles	HOUR	10	11	12	1	2	3	4	5	6	7	8
—	The Dyke.......dep.	39	37	36	46	38	38	37	37	37	37	50
3	Rowan Halt G.......	48	46	45	55	47	47	46	46	46	46	1
3¼	Aldrington Halt.....	50	49	48	58	50	50	49	50	49	49	4
4	Hove................	53	51	51	0	52	52	51	52	51	53	6
4½	Holland Road Halt..	55	53	.	2	54	54	54	54	53	56	8
5¼	Brighton ....arr.	59	57	.	6	58	58	58	58	57	0	12

E Except Sats. G Rowan Halt for Elm Drive. S Sats. only.

OTHER TRAINS between Brighton and Aldrington Halt, page 219.

Tickets from the G.R.Croughton Collection

Closure

With traffic falling steadily away for some years, the future of the line was looking very bleak and it came as no great surprise when the Southern Railway announced that they were going to close it. The final day of service was on Saturday December 31st 1938 and on the front page of the Monday January 2nd 1939 issue of the *Sussex Daily News* the final trip by train to the Dyke Station (pulled by E4 class 0-6-0T No.2505) was described as follows:-

TRAIN'S LAST RUN TO THE DYKE

NEARLY 400 PASSENGERS ON FINAL TRIP

BUSY TEN MINUTES AT JOURNEY'S END

Fog Signals, Farewells and Auld Lang Syne

CLOSED FOR WANT OF CUSTOM

Few railwaymen have the privilege of closing down a railway line, or even a wayside station, but to Porter Charles John Weller, signalman, ticket collector, booking clerk, porter and "stationmaster" at the Devil's Dyke, this duty fell on Saturday as he locked up and joined the 5.27 to Brighton.

In spite of agitation by residents of the more populous districts on the Brighton-Dyke railway, the line has now been closed down, and the Southern Railway has said that it is all due to "lack of support."

For fifty years the "Dyke Express" has carried people out to the Devil's Dyke and the surrounding Downs, but it will run no more.

The stations, halts and track are to be dismantled, and already the work of pulling up the tiny goods yards at the Dyke terminus has been commenced.

So, on Saturday evening, people who make a habit of being present when little slices of history are made, booked to the Dyke for 8½d. (cheap day return) on the 5.7 p.m. from Brighton. At the Dyke they got out and walked about while Porter Weller shifted the points, clipped the tickets, and shunted the engine to take the 5.27 back to Brighton - the "Ghost Train" of the Dyke Railway.

Mr.F.T.Roach, the Brighton Stationmaster, complete in his top hat, took with him destination boards for the return trip -'Journey's End' they read," writes a "Sussex Daily News" reporter who made the last trip, and "scooped" the souvenir hunters for the last ticket!

As the 5.7 steamed out to the Dyke the engines in the Brighton repair sheds screamed their farewells, fog signals crashed out their contributions to the finale. All along the 5½ miles route more passengers joined in the historic journey, and at each stop more fog signals echoed as the "Express" chugged off on its way to the Dyke. People in houses adjoining the line drew back their blinds and waved; at each stop there were sightseers to cheer the train on to the end of its run.

Four coaches and a saloon made the trip, and nearly 400 passengers will cherish their ticket as a souvenir of the run.

Auld Lang Syne

At the Dyke, Porter Weller had the busiest ten minutes of his 20 years in the service of the Company. He had to serve tickets, uncouple the engine, change the signals, alter the points, blow out the oil lamps and lock up for the last time.

And as he turned the last key he was greeted with music of Auld Lang Syne. Passengers joined in the singing, musicians in the saloon made merry, paper hats and streamers - relics of Christmas - made their appearance.

But even for the last run some effort has to be made to schedule and at 5.47 just ten minutes late, the guard waved his flag, the "Express" tooted its farewell to the Downs, fifty fog signals and cheering and shouting passengers gave her a great send off, and Porter Weller, with his oil lamp still smoking, took a last look at his outpost.

For nine years Porter Weller has filled his many roles at the Dyke Station, his lonely post on the Sussex Downs, which are deserted in the winter and thronged in the summer time. Often the trains he greeted from Brighton have been passengerless, sometimes a stray parcel or two have found their way up to the lonely Dyke residents, but now the "Express" runs no more and Dyke folk must get to and from Brighton by bus.

A Daily Passenger

Mrs. Saunders, who lives close to the Station, will miss the "Express." For seven years she has gone daily to and from Brighton to fetch her meat, her bread and her groceries, for her Stores only deliver at the Dyke once a fortnight!

The Dyke railway has been losing traffic for years in the winter time because the last train from Brighton is the 5.7 p.m. In summer time there is a later service, and this suits the Dyke folk, but in winter time they must forsake the trains and travel on the buses.

Porter Weller will be found fresh work at Hove, but sympathy must go out to Mrs. Saunders - for now that the 9.10 a.m. does not run she will not get her morning paper until the postman calls the following day!

Normally the 5.37 flashes through the Golf Club "station" built for the benefit of the members of the Brighton and Hove Golf Club, but on Saturday it stopped for two passengers, making the trip on it with their plus fours and golf bags for the last time.

First and Last

One passenger to make the trip was Mr. Bob Pitt, a well known Brightonian who made the first trip in 1887.

Now after fifty-one years of service the Dyke Express will run no more.

Five miles of track will have to be pulled up, platforms have to be demolished, and the line which winds its way through the Downs will vanish.

Porter Weller has set his signals for the last train. . . . .

In actual fact, three more trains ran from Brighton to Rowan Halt on that day, the final train being worked by D1 class 0-4-2T No.2699 which left Brighton at 8.00 p.m. and returned from Rowan Halt at 8.31 p.m.

Some of the passengers making merry on the last run to the Dyke Station and back on December 31st 1938. Sussex Daily News

E4 class 0-6-2T No.2505 en-route to the Dyke Station with a single carriage.

The late O.J.Morris / Lens of Sutton

The Present Scene

After closure the track was removed around 1939/40, so very little remains to remind or show people that a railway line ever ran up the towards the Devils Dyke.

Aldrington Halt is still open on the main Brighton to Portsmouth line, but from the junction as far as Old Shoreham Road, the route is buried under business development and a petrol station. The girder bridge at Old Shoreham Road, which crossed over the line was filled in, and the road routed over it. For many years there was a kink in the road where the bridge lay underneath, but during the 1970's the bridge was dug up and the road levelled out to its present form.

Further business development and the Hove Fire Station are built on the site of the embankment, north of the road. From here the route is still quite visible although no trace of Rowan Halt which was situated behind Rowan Avenue, can be seen. A recreation ground and school cover the area north of here until the point where the railway crossed Hangleton Road

The 40 ft embankment which carried the railway over the bridge at both Hangleton Road and West Way has long since been removed. The Hangleton Road bridge was removed in 1940 and the road itself being raised to its present level and widened in 1942. The headstone from the bridge is in Hangleton Manor Public House and is dated 1885. The bridge over West Way was removed in 1943. The Northease Drive bridge and cutting each side were filled with Hove's wartime concrete tank traps in March 1943. The cutting was later infilled to the present road level, while the bridge itself was removed in 1949.

From here the whole area is now cut into two, with the introduction of the dual carriageway of the A27 trunk-road although beyond this point the route of the former railway becomes a public footpath called "The Dyke Railway Trail" until just short of the site of Golf Club Halt which is covered by undergrowth. From here the route is very overgrown and is out of bounds to walkers.

The site of the former Dyke Station is now the Devil's Dyke Farm and is on private property. All the station buildings have been removed and replaced with farm buildings, although a short section of the platform is still visible.

The Dyke Hotel was destroyed by fire in 1945 but was rebuilt as a restaurant in 1954 and has since been refurbished, while very little remains of the steep grade railway or the aerial cableway to show anyone that they ever existed.

The remains of the Dyke Station platform on April 21st 2000. Author

Conclusion

There is no doubt that the Dyke branch line was built with the very best intentions, and during the summer months was of great value to the people of Brighton and their visitors who wanted to travel to the Devil's Dyke and its attractions at the Dyke Hotel. Unfortunately for the railway, times change and surprisingly the line only lasted just over fifty one years. If it had actually reached the Dyke Hotel it may have lasted a bit longer, and if it still existed today, it would no doubt be a great attraction.

The branch to the Dyke has long past into history but will always fascinate railway historians and enthusiasts alike because of its very unique nature.

Looking back, one wonders what that very distinguished company of officials and visitors who gathered in the rain at the Dyke Station for the formal opening in 1887 would say today if they could only see what has happened to the Dyke railway. After all their light hearted comments about the Devil, maybe some of the gathering could be forgiven for thinking that he might well have had the last laugh.

Acknowledgements

I would like to thank the following people and organisations for their kind help in compiling information and supplying photographs for this publication: Mr.R.C.Riley, Mr.G.Dinnage, Mr.B.R.Hart, Mr.R.M.Casserley (for the H.C.Casserley photographs), Mr.G.Jacobs, Mr.G.R.Croughton, Mr.R.F.Roberts, Mr.S.Berry (from Hangleton) for all his "on the spot" information, the librarians and staff at Brighton Library and also Hove Library, the Public Records Office at Kew, the East Sussex Public Records Office at Lewes, and last but certainly not least the late Mr.J.L.Smith of Lens of Sutton.

My thanks as always to James Christian of Binfield Printers Ltd.

Bibliography

THE RAILWAYS OF DEVIL'S DYKE by Paul Clark (Turntable Publications)
FORGOTTEN RAILWAYS: SOUTH-EAST ENGLAND by H.P.White (David & Charles)
THE RAILWAYS OF SOUTHERN ENGLAND: SECONDARY AND BRANCH LINES by Edwin Course (Batsford)
SOUTHERN RAILWAY BRANCH LINE TRAINS by R.W.Kidner (Oakwood Press)
RAILWAY MAGAZINE (The Devil's Dyke Railway by Frank S. White. March 1939)
THE MODEL RAILWAY NEWS (Railway Topics by J.N.Maskelyne. February 1939)

Happier days at the Dyke Station as E4 class 0-6-2T No.2497 prepares to leave with a four carriage train.
G.A.Strickler